Write-Handed Poetry

A Collection of Thoughts and Writings on Faith, Family, Love, Sex, Revolution, and Blackness

A. Denèe

For Leslie

For Detroit

Cover and photography by: Ashley Wallace

Contents

II
THE MIRROR BEHIND EYES

III

FLIPPING THROUGH BLANK PAGES, DIGGING UP THE UNACCOUNTED

ACKNOWLEDGEMENTS

I thank God for anointing my hands to write. Only the Lord knows how much life and death, pain and laughter that went into every word in this book— my blessing. *Write-Handed Poetry* exists as an homage to my sister Leslie, who will always be the brightest light in my heart and work. Love: You are my muse. Thank you for your creative genius, sweet love, and extra eyeballs. Mama and Daddy: You two are God's fingerprints. Thank you for giving me a high five with every dream and aspiration. Mama, you always make me feel special and capable. Daddy, I appreciate all of our debates on everything under the sun. My parents and siblings are my greatest cheerleaders; whether I write poetry or cure a disease. Wenona: You are a brilliant and beautiful big sister. John: You are a walking miracle and the silliest big brother. I was born into the flyyest, craziest crew of aunts, uncles, and cousins. I appreciate all of you and the excitement that everyone had when I decided to publish. Y'all are there when I need my village most. To my 7 heartbeats: Taylor, LaNard, Jalen, Johnny, Michael, Jordan, and Bryce: You all are on my mind every moment that I breathe. You bring me joy.

Cat: Always Truthfully Perfected, always sisters, always friends. Jocelyn: You know all of my poems. Because you are a true friend and motivator, I gained the courage to take writing seriously. Dr. April Bell: You got stuck with me when I was a bashful high school kid and are still down. Academia is a better place because you're in it. Thank you for taking education outside of the classroom. Dr. Margaret Jordan: Your kindness, grace, and brilliance stretched my mind and sparked my love for English! Your knowledge and wisdom opened my eyes. Dr. Ongiri: You will never know how much you built me up. Miss Faye: For including me in the REVOLUTION! You are my Yoda.

Special Thanks To: Big Nard, Mama Ophelia, Ashley Wallace and the Mellow Soul Squadd, Cheryl, Denise, Pat, Vee, Davie, Sammy, Bonnie Brown, Alba, Ronald E. McNair Scholars at Wayne State University and Dr. Joseph B., Upward Bound, April (my tight end), Chris, Nina, Becky, Christian, Avery, Alpha Omega, Hilary (Thank you for still reaching out and being a sister), New Jerusalem MBC, Dr. Gordon, Dr. Watts, Dr. Treece, Dr. Mosby, Dr. Rogers, Nola Grey, Rose, and all my students who always educate me. I am truly grateful for Dr. Nikki Giovanni for graciously sharing divine wisdom and encouragement with me. Meeting you changed my life. Huge shout out to my "home away from home" folks in Gainesville and Jacksonville, Florida.

A POEM TO THE READER

"The Recipe to Write-Handed Poetry"

Layer'd
my blackness
my phatness
like ripe, green-peppered memories
simmering with tender onion-type stories
Tears of glee and misery fall upon . . .

Layer'd
Psalms and anointing of heads
Choir robes and sick beds
like violet laced cloths upon dresses, deemed too short
like the whimpered prayer before the abort

Layer'd
With mommas and daddies who dance together still
With wills already done and promises fulfilled
loving the black boys returning from stores
loving the brown girls just learning to speak English
lovers together,
forty plus, "post-crush"
loving rush hours that come right on time

Layer'd
The mystery of glossy book covers
flyy brothers and society's "others"
learning how to read
how to crease yellowed gems
packed with words from busy craniums

like traffic on a Friday
like liquor on a Sunday

Writing poetry is icing...
Life is cake...

Don't jump while it's cookin'
...then you may taste

"Just for today, I'm telling the truth like it's going out of style"
India.Arie

WRITE-HANDED POETRY

A COLLECTION OF THOUGHTS AND WRITINGS ON FAITH, FAMILY, LOVE, SEX, REVOLUTION, AND BLACKNESS

I

POETRY WRITTEN ABOVE THE CLOUDS AND BETWEEN HEAVEN

What a Day

What a day for love,
Since yesterday didn't get so much of it.
I have to apologize to myself for that
But, today is my day for love.
And the one I'm loving...

The Heart of a Woman

Love can be written upon the greatest of tablets,
Recorded for the most remarkable of records,
but when the shelter in which it resided
has been pierced
and begins to leak from its very life source,
A new creation has been formed

The broken heart of a woman is her most mortal self
It is invisible, she cannot see what she feels
But she is feeling
This is her regret

Destroying the heart that she once knew
The heart that first allowed love to fill its walls
The heart that once loved you

Dear Heart

Let the clouds form now
Because my heart is breaking
And we are not one

Breathe You
For Red

Here is a pact that I make with self:
That I will live unselfishly
That I will exist as an assistant to your life
From my heart,
I'd never deceive you
Sister, I breathe you
If I could just wrap my arms around your weakness
I'd hold you with all my strength
And just to let you know,
I wouldn't dare let go
Until all that I have has empowered you to go on
Enveloped your being so tight,
I squeeze
Until greatness bursts out,
Just breathe
If there exists any fear or doubt,
I would whisper the knowledge and wisdom
Of fore lived generations in your ears,
Secrets from past years,
So that your future may be secured.
Rest assured, that I can't move on
Until you're ahead
So I can look at your shadow and cover myself in your greatness.
Revive those who pass us in the backwards walk
Bless those who are bound by defeatist talk
Oh my sister if I could just breathe you
I'd love you
Before you could even feel unloved
I'd hug you
Before someone unworthy of your touch does it for me
I'd encourage you
But I know that it's hard
And life can pierce a healed heart
With no remorse
Put a detour
On victory's course
But sister, just let me breathe you
So maybe I'd understand why you just settle

7

Why my vision isn't clear enough to see your pain
And my hearing isn't good enough to hear your cries
What I think are lies
Is really the truth in disguise
And I just don't know it
Please, I beg you, show it
I miss the bliss of our talking
All night dreaming, impacting the world while sleep walking
I don't want to go back
Time can't take the trip
But it's the future that I look forward to
And at the same time dread
Can't shake my thoughts of you being dead
Of your spirit in turmoil while I move ahead
So I stop what I'm doing
Because I'm dying here
Can't breathe until I breathe you
Put faith back into your being
Praying that prayer keeps you strong
If you pray still
Myself I'd kill
If you'd be healed
Sister, I'm praying
That's the most I can do,
But lately it's too hard
to think about you
So I can't hide my hurt from your hurt
PLEASE JUST LET ME SEE WHY YOU SETTLE
Why dwell in the middle of mediocrity's mediocre contentment
Enrage yourself to excel
Fight those who donned you POW
Break out that cell and battle
Destroy the hell that's surrounding you
By reaching up for Heaven and taking a piece of God with you
And when He's in you
Sister, let me breathe you
So God can give me the ability to trust Him
To walk with you
Let that peace in God flow throughout your veins and fill your heart with
the wholeness
That no one else knew to teach you

I don't preach to you,
Since I lost the words to say
But I'm finding profound wisdom in silence
Calm as my violence
And peace as my kill
Don't swallow that pill of corruption
Destruction will always follow
Because life's just like that
End your sorrow by loving yourself
I can't love you more than that,
Though many people say they can,
I'll love you differently than man,
I'll give you the love that I have for myself
And let your heart love the rest
Flow through your breast
And exhale
So that I can breathe you
Not needing a situational sister
But one who's there until our Father
Gives either one the keys
to a private mansion
Paradise for eternity
Just send the invitation,
What a divine house party
But your world hasn't ended yet
You could still use a friend
In yourself
Just befriend such a queen
And she'll make raindrops of golden guidance fall upon your face
Know that those storm clouds are containing only the best for you
So don't wish them away
Dance in the darkness, because it can't stand your glee
Light is soon to come, but it can't stand misery
So just breathe
Breathe, my sister
Breathe
And I will breathe you
Back into yourself,
To make sure you never forget
How precious your every breath is

3 Generations
For mothers

Tears bursting with depression and hopelessness escape my eyes
And fall on the altar
Where my mother laid her burdens
And my grandmother laid her husband
And five children
To rest.

Diamante's Offspring

Music
Tranquil, emotional
Singing, performing, dancing
Tours, records, stanzas, haikus
Writing, thinking, speaking
Visual, audio
Poetry

You Are

God, You are aesthetic.
After trading Your Son's life for me,
God, You are prolific.

You are poetic

In the same magnitude of trees and snow, mountains and rain,
You collect pieces of pain
Create peace of mind
During wilderness times
And encounters with devious kinds
You welcome me as friend.

You are artistic.

Simplistic enough to create molecules, complex enough to make them
essential to the most complicated.

You are my everything
Don't have everything

God, You are my All

Save Me

Worship
for
Eternity
Enter
Broken
To fully
Complete
Serenity
Conscious divinity
Threshing
Learning
Burning
Transform
Pure
And
New
And
Whole

Untitled

They're sitting, anxiously awaiting to receive my, I mean Your ministry. Every line written, profound. With every stanza, every rhyme, I'm sweet. Throw in some inferences and I'm deep. But God, hear my prayer and make this poem about You. I don't want to be sugar, sweetening the taste buds of people. Make me salt, so that after I'm done, they are thirsty for You. I'm thirsty too, so reign and hydrate me with Your dew. I can't make my poetry sweet, but I can make it about you.

Ode to Friend

Growing to know you became an adventure
As seasons changed and we aged,
So did our minds: for better or for worse

We distanced at the divide
And the road split too far for us
Though we still connected,
my road moved on, yours headed to end

I regret not calling back, the rings now a silent hum
I regret not reaching out, my time seemed too chaotic
For an old friend

Why didn't I invest more into your life?
Why did I criticize often and pray less?
Words worthless as you kiss death.

And I live
And I write
And I life

Please rest
As we sleep
And meet in the clouds

Let us dance upon the skies
I will bring your daughter
Just to let her hug daddy once more

Restoration for mother
For sister
For brother
For all things that passed away

for her first born
young departed

Grass

Threaded upon the Earth's face, I grow upward towards bliss
Reaching for Deity, bowing before the Sun
As glory rests, I am restored
I am renewed
I am complete
Through the seasons of cold and bitter, hot and stormy,
I touch heaven still
I look up
God's splendor falls all around a world that knows not, but exists
because of.
And all I want is to sit beside the still waters
And all I want
And All
Peace

Sonnet 1: Lovely, Divine

How can I love thee perfectly,
When I am flesh and my heart deceive
You are the breath of mountain and sea:
Your magnificence beyond what minds conceive.

Surround me with Your nature and I live,
Complete and secure that You are my love.
Upon my lips, total adoration I give.
Blow, my air. Stand, my tree. Fly, my dove.

I long to please You, though often I fail.
Daily, I think of ways to improve.
You, my waters, I drink from Your well.
This thirst insatiable, no other may remove.

Open my eyes so that Christ is my sight,
For loving You perfectly is my eternal plight.

Poem #1

You are art perfected
I am humbled
And seek more of Your Inhabitance
Unite with me so that I may be whole

What a beautiful treasure
What an everlasting melody
What a Divine connection

I write for You.
Stand for rights with You.
My love, o how I adore.
My love, o how I adore.

Please touch me,
Hold my hand,
Embrace me,
Love.

Send me a poem in the clouds
And call it rain.
Paint me a portrait on earth
And call it family.
My breath is You.
Your words design me.
Your love defines me.
Captivate me.

Your nature is song
I am captured
It's just the two of us
So let's dance forever.

Poem #2

Your mercy is a wondrous
Regal gift
I lift my head to seek Your face

I clear my mind so that I may experience
Heaven on Earth

To Maude Martha
Inspired by Gwendolyn Brooks

Yellow jewels garnish your emerald grounds,
Mounds of salt, extracted from your sapphire tears, pound my heart,
They pound my heart.
Your "yella" fella kisses your coffee-colored lips,
And pulls that long "knappy" hair during orgasmic trips,
While you dream in jade.

The subtle smells of ginger and sweet potato pie
Flies throughout your kitchenette, luring creeping things
They lure creeping things.
Day meetings with the red-brown, high yellow, low yellow women, teach within
Beauty lessons, golden rules on why to bleach your skin.

Holidays and gatherings culminate misery,
History reminds you of shame socially.
Pink noses, red cheeks, speak lowly of the cocoa faces.
They speak slowly to cocoa faces.

But at least you still have your long hair and sweet potato pie

I am not Fish
December 31, 2009

Watching,
Looking,
Moving in your container,
Contained.

Swimming in circles,
Moving nowhere.
Watching,
Looking
At others preoccupied,
Awaiting to be fed.

Through your glass,
a distorted vision.
I open my eyes
Never knew how to swim.
Never could stay shallow.
Launch me out in the deep,
And I'll walk on water,
My faith is cool like that.

Cast your nets, I won't be in that school,
I rule the waters and travel as one.
Ask me to swim with limits
And my hearing impairs.
The music in my life is too loud,
I'm proud.

I am not Fish

I am when I grow up,
Higher than a dream,
Mingling with the heavens,
I create new worlds.
Words cannot script my future,
I am not your design.

Designate my actions,
And I'll redefine motion.
Commotion about my life,
Be silenced.

I am not Fish

I am clay to the Almighty,
Refined by fire,
I transcend earth's elements,
Opposition to the tide,
A threat to the enemy.
I am my destiny,
Inspired by divinity,
I am me.

Not Fish.

Poem #3

Eyes closed,
body pressed against body…
Penis enter tight opening…
Sweating…
Pushing…
Hurting…
But…
Pushing…
Moaning…
Tic…
Toc…
And minutes later…
Life

Obligatorily placed in murk

In company of dirt
And creeping things

Swept under the living room rug. . .

          Our only family heirloom

City, State, Country

"City, State and Country please..."
       New Orleans, Michigan, Haiti

New Orleans

The Big Easy, easily recognized by Satchmo and the Queen of Gospel,
Mother Jackson
Fashioned on Bourbon and jazzin' on the French Quarter.
See, this good ole boy deceived us po' boys to believin' that we was
conceivin' something beautiful
Magically, our purples and reds, oranges and yellows mellowed down to
browns, blacks and dead,
Yet you expect us to pledge
To red, white and blue
My city is built upon walls that was built upon walls of deprivation
Elevation of the waters didn't cause a cause, but because of the fall
We've fallen into muddy waters
Our sons and daughters are slaughtered in the Super Dome
And home is a ragged pad submerged in wet earth.
Giving birth to the truth, circumcising this baby called justice.
She's malnourished, nourishing her residue for the population of few.
Who shall I pledge allegiance to?
To the Ninth Ward, now the None Ward?
To the homes now boats, afloat blood, sweat and tears?
Been years
And I've found the real weapons of mass destruction and they're called:
FEMA
Home Owner's insurance and
The United States of America

"City, State and Country please..."
       New Orleans, Michigan, Haiti

Michigan

The Wolverine State has been hunted down, chopped up and served for
dinner
And the winner is.... No one
Production of cars was our business,

couldn't fit us in your business
cause we were the owners.
Now go to your local gas station and the guy asking for a buck is
probably the engineer of your car.
How far have we gotten when the government is plottin' to give funds to
others, ignoring the burden pressed upon this state
We are in a state of emergency, but all of our celebrities are giving distant
countries their "charity"
Close enough for admirers to praise and see…
Far enough to elude energy and sincerity…
          WHERE IS OUR RELIEF?
Please put our children at ease, while all of our jobs are overseas,
                           …and the Big 3
are three of the greatest PIMPS in Michigan history.
Let's not even address the distress in DPS.
I mean Motorcity has money in the inner city
while "The Motor City" is worth less than a third world country.
Please don't insult me
We've got U of D and Wayne State University
Universally, institutions that institute tuitions
as if their students were wealthy.
How can they have EFCs
when families need to eat
And I can't grasp the Black student retention rate,
Racially speaking, the number of minority college drop outs are
increasing, increasingly decreasing first-generation college graduates
Pushing us to ask Auntie Sallie Mae for thousands, payin' her back more
than double
Our state is in trouble
When there are more kids who can't read than enslaved Africans during
slavery,
More unemployment than the resources to solve it
There is no office to return to,
We are all broke,
Choking on these contaminated fluids leaking from the Greats Lakes,
Drowning in debt

"City, State and Country please…"
      New Orleans, Michigan, Haiti

Haiti

1804

1

8

0

4

The first time in world history, we have a free black country
Free for blacks, Africans and Latinos
For decades, escalading to poverty and national urgency
Before you see that shaken earth,
we must see the prior disaster in Haiti.
Sickness and Disease went ignored by the public eye
Please tell me why,
Stationed as our ancestors, disowned by our selfish present
The representative of the unspoken
Came with the high G.P.A of 7.0.
Started low, but Now we know what Haiti needs,
Bleeds for amputees, death toll growin,
Who planted these seeds?
See this Re-Fu-Gee tried to tell us
To care about our Haitian Brothas
And sistahs, he was Gone til November
But we didn't listen until January
Bury over 200,000 in unmarked graves
To a free nation when we were slaves
But we be free
Free we be
Be we free
Liberty
Tell
 Me
Tell
Me
Haiti
Free

"City, State and Country…Please"

White Sea

I never knew how to swim
I never knew how to coordinate arms and legs
Move at such a pace that my body would resist against the force of water
I never knew how to swim

I thought I could at least hold my breath
Take in the air above me and keep it in as I submerged
What I imagined to be minutes were merely 10, 12, 14 seconds
I thought I could at least hold my breath

I was always too scared to open my eyes
Because the fear of my inabilities stunned me
I did not want to see my failed attempts at survival
I was always too scared to open my eyes

In this white sea, I exist alone
So used to safe rivers and streams
That I did not realize that I was headed towards rip currents
In this white sea, I exist alone

A small existence of hope dwells within me
For I feel the waters choking me
Rushing around and forcing itself upon me with all its vastness
A small existence of hope dwells within me

My eyes are fixed on the Lord
As I try to swim and hold my breath at once
Alone, stinging and fighting to live beyond existence
My eyes are fixed on the Lord

Getaway My Love

Let us get away
Fly above the clouds
In Heaven, You stay
I'll take Your hand and we'll

Getaway

Walking upon the ocean's face
Gazing in the eyes of my Love
The stars of Your heart, I'll trace
Lines that connect I to You

Getaway

And lie together in peace,
Resting in the arms of wholeness
My inhaling has ceased
You take my breath away

Getaway

Into a field of creams and greens
The scent of You surround
The place of my deepest dreams
For we dance together in our

Getaway

To Beauty
To Paradise
To Utopia
To Laughter
To Joy
To Perfection
To You

My love

Hemoglobin

I am sick of selling these sickle cells to blue crosses and blue shields,
Yielding my body to painful injections, artificial deflections of reality,
Cause in reality, they can't get me high enough
to forget that my hemoglobin is low enough for a transfusion.
Dear bone marrow: As you push out those crimson quarter moons,
save room for some normal ones.
Please save room for some normal ones.

I am sick of selling these sickle cells to "We're-gonna-have-to-keep-you"
blues . . .
Play that guitar baby, as I moan a little longer.
Well, at least until the medicine kicks in,
ending my lucidity, ability to groove to the tunes from the illest music
The illest movements happen in these veins,
While I vainly wish that it wasn't me.

I am sick of selling these sickle cells to self-consciousness,
unconsciousness full of hapless helplessness
Less of this could possibly cure this illness,
If the apathy did not seem endless.
Convince me that thriving and living will never be synonymous,
Consistently reminding me that this too shall pass
Crises, too must pass
These, too, will pass

I am sick of selling these sickle cells to abstract ideas of health
Wealth could treat me . . . if I was wealthy,
Health would please me . . . if I was healthy,
But I am the forgotten cell.
The-SC-versus-SS-cell.
The are-you-sure-you-don't-have-the-trait cell.
The how-long-have-you-had-this cell
The what-does-it-feel-like cell
The ask-those-dumb-questions-to-my-pain cell.
Plainly sale your redundancy, by asking me to rate my pain,
Why don't *you* pick a number?

I am sick of selling these sickle cells to warm compresses and Icy Hots
Rubbing out knots in my arms and legs, back and hips.

Impressed when I go through to a painless month,
Blessed when I make it a year,
Praying that I make it a lifetime
Praying that I make it a lifetime

Wailing Floor

Her spirit visits me in the darkness,
Nightmares of piss and feces and blood-lined sputum.
She speaks to me
And recalls cold, loveless nights.
Emotionally, she remembers those somber weeks of 1825.

Tiny slits appear on my knees,
Infected
And stigmata-like:
Divinely transferred suffering.
That intimate kiss between human flesh and wooden floors
Are fervent prayers guised as housework

Shadows of those still bodies
Shadows of those still bodies

Poetic Proposal

Marry me poetry
And I will be yours forever
Let us make metaphoric love
And simultaneously orgasm, shuttering similes
While sweating seductive, sensual alliterations

Take this figurative ring
And we will share our love through
Biblical times
Medieval times
Romantic times
Victorian times
Jacobian times
Modern times
Post-modern times
African times
Slavery antebellum times
New Negro times
Civil Rights times
Radical times
Hip-hop times
All through time

Marry me poetry
And we will make slam babies
And free verse babies
And haiku babies
And Petrarchan sonnet babies
And English sonnet babies
And acrostic babies
And corona babies
And epic babies
And concrete babies
And ballad babies
And lyric babies
And color babies
We will rock the cradle and rule the literary world

Just say "I do"

And I promise a life full of rhythms and rhymes,
Pentameters and personifications
Allusions and allegories
Hyperboles and homonyms
Imageries and idioms
Metonyms and motifs

Together, we could be the perfect couplet
Please me with your meters
And I'll make breakfast in the morning

Marry me poetry
And I will write poems for you
Poems to you
And we will be two joined as one
You, the art form
And I, the poet

Heavenly Patterns

God,
You are the quatrain in my soul's Italian sonnet
A-B-B-A
Father

I'll Be John Brown
For Mama Ophelia

Mama hit 100
And daddy died young
But mama hit 100
Before her life was done

Daddy was a good man
So I ain't down
Try'n say otherwise,
I'll be John Brown

Mama said, "Chile' I'll tell you,
Listen to what I say
Honey, I tell you
The Lawd's comin' back someday"

I listened to mama
I ain't no clown
Call her a lie,
I'll be John Brown

With my husband, done had 10 young,
Taught 'em 'bout God
Taught 10 young
Ain't never spared the rod

We chastised them
Gave out whippin's by the pound
Call that child abuse,
I'll be John Brown

Thanks to my young, got me 27 grand
Done lost a lot of loved ones
We done had our ups and downs

Ma still don't make no promises
I don't play around
I mis sayin'
I'll be John Brown

35

Day Dreaming Hero

I struggle with my decisions and positions. Position myself as the
metaphoric, pseudo-savior. I write about it to
                                   fight about it,
                                                 doing nothing about it,

                                                          unless they read about it.

Nip
For Whitney

Dancing Souls, they take the stage and bow before your royalty,
They curtsy for your royalty
Then you open your mouth and the angels in heaven are jealous.
They envy your voice.
You stand and the world stops for one moment in time.
For one moment of time, countries dare to declare peace,
People blinded by superficial chasms, open their eyes for the first time
So that they may see how stunning you are.
And those dancing souls dance.

They surround your presence and applaud in awe of your legacy.
You legendarily dismantled the standards and called Heaven the limit
You produced colors, o the beautiful colors that escaped from your
fingertips
Every time you touched a microphone,
Every time you touched a Dancing Soul.

Even now, you sing to us. You impress us.
And yes, even now your story is an eternal melody
For those Dancing Souls
Who are entranced by your bravery
Your strength in error and humility in triumph.

I hear your song and Dancing Souls step to your tune.
They glide,
They shake,
They groove,
They simply move,
As you have moved our Dancing Souls.

Breathe You II

Here is a pact that I make with self:
That I will recommit myself to your freedom.
Strap on new wings, when the old ones fail you
Because gravity has never failed to pull you down,
Drowned you in an intangible marine.
So when you have grown weary,
Try to breathe
And taste second wind

Seeping in your soul, renewing your faith,
For I know you've become faithless.
Rebuilding your hope,
Because you seem to be hopeless.
Perfecting strength divinely,
Beyond "not enough,"
Prepare your lungs
As I breathe you
To a place where bondage cannot bind you,
Where darkness cannot find you,
Where only love surrounds you.

Sister, I plea
Relinquish struggle's torment and breathe with me.
Together, we will inhale liberty, autonomy, and self-esteem.
Consistently, I will release divinity, for you are spirit.
Spiritually, I will speak to your heart in different tongues,
Revive precious memories of when we were young
Enough to live simply,
Simple enough to love blindly,
And blind enough to see God clearly.
When the natural became invisible, unable to block our vision,
Unable to create division.
When you opened your mouth
To let God breathe in you
And when She's begun, let me breathe you too

Because, Sister, you are strong.
But for too long, you've renounced your strength.
You allowed the world's weight to break you,

Broken, you allowed brokenness to change you.
So I must breathe you
To incite your healing.
The wounds have festered for far too long
beneath the external subterfuge,
Masquerading before your layered mind,
Kindly protecting "family business,"
Constantly refracting from urgent business.
But it is my business to exhale,
Because you are suffocating.
Hyperventilating since your life became a vacuum.
So inhale my donation of air before you are consumed.
This is all I can do
Breathe you to a place high enough
For your hero to find you,
Rescue you from yourself.
Because the hero is you, but the villain is too
So I will breathe you until you can choose

But Sister, you must choose
Strive, fight, press
Stand tall, puff out your chest.
Become the woman that you've never met.
Though she's seen you, life caused a disconnect
Reconnect with God and She will help you identify her,
Return to your native self and embrace the future
And if you find yourself too captive to be free,
Come to me,
And
Remember to
breathe

If you just let me,
I will breathe you too.
I will breathe with you
And promise to never leave you breathless
Again.

II

THE MIRROR BEHIND EYES

Mastered Body

Last night, I touched myself.
Resisting at first, I felt my left hand slowly creep under my lace and
embrace the curves of my behind. Gently, squeeze.
Gently, breathe
out all the anxieties I felt as I touched myself.
Enjoyed the quest before me, exploring myself. Feeling my hands roam
around a body in appreciation, in homage. Hands deserving of such a
treasure. A treasure deserving of curiosity and pleasure.

Last night, as my palm rubbed my belly upwards and collided with the
softness of my breasts, I exhaled.
Amazed at how far I allowed this pursuit go to, I felt my nipples harden
and rise as I tickled them between my fingers.
Breathe . . .
breathe . . .
I knew where this was headed. I knew that once I had given every inch of
my body its proper attention, I could feel the eager river of anticipation
splashing against my thighs.
So almost magnetically, I was pulled towards the center of my body, to
feel the warmth and moisture that covered it.

It was then that I understood the male obsession, the societal fear, the
female shame. This place was beautiful, thus my entrancement;
mysterious, thus my fright; foreign, thus my awkwardness.

But in spite of myself, despite myself, I craved more, yearned for a
deeper revelation. I desired to learn of the most sensual lessons, only
received from this delicate, humble, exciting, teacher. So slowly, I moved
my fingertips around my clitoris. As it swelled, I entered the gateway of
my body. I searched for spots never touched before and found them.
Breathe . . .
breathe . . .
My fingertips moved quicker, pressed more firmly and my hips began to
groove to silent tunes of uncontained, unwritten, unsung bliss. Fingers,
nipples, behind, vulva, belly, thighs… all moved simultaneously in
unrehearsed motions.
In, outtttt…
Breathe…
Circle, circle, quickly…

41

bre . .

brea. . .

My mind floated, my entire being lifted into the air.

Breathe . . . and then . . . my muscles stiffened in preparation for . . . .
breathe . . . my toes coiled tightly . . my . . . my stomach . . . my legs . . .
and then . . . I quivered. . . breathless, I shook . . . my body presented me
with the forbidden . . . the rarest gift unknown to man . . . gasping for air,
every muscle inside of me trembled. And I melted into the threads of my
sheets, awestruck at this quest now conquered.

This moment unfathomably experienced.

Last night, I touched myself and discovered orgasm.
I discovered woman. I captured beauty. Forced nothing, pleased
everything and my skin tingles at the memory. Satisfaction given and
received, all in one lovely stroke. And the smile upon my face was
returned between my thighs. We thanked each other for the introduction,
long overdue

With the promise of meeting again…

Cancer: A Series of Short Poems

i

Spirit. Body. Blood. Cell. Cancer. Life. Uncertain. Love. Love.

ii

Red moons revolve. Pink sun centered. Sun don't set. Please don't set. Red moons bleed. Dripping crimson tears. Into a black sea. Sun dry these tears. Drink from this sea. Black. Red. Sun don't set. Please don't set. Enter me and inject your sunshine into my soul. Red moon revolve. My mind swirling. I cry red tears, my brown skin stained. Rebel against memory. I desire to behold you forever. Take my soul. Take my body and leave your pink rays in the black sea. Leave rays in the black sea.

iii

Today, I'm gonna flip cancer the bird. I'm gonna take this chemo and shove it in my veins, then take this chemo and shove it up cancer's ass. Today, I woke up and said to cancer, "fuck off."

iv

Machine beeps . . . beep . . . occlusion . . . beep . . . beep . . . "Please try to keep your arm straight" . . . stale air . . . dry vomit upon the corners of her mouth . . . "Drink something" . . . beep beep beep . . . "Just turn that damn sound off" . . . cold liquid flows through her veins . . . burning . . . cold . . . burning . . . . beep . . . beep . . . beep . . . "If I had a dime for every time that thing beeps" . . . "If I had an extra year every time that . . . beeeeep . . . beeeeeep . . . beeeeped"

New Year (For 2012)

This year, I resolve nothing.

For the eve of this year was spent inside of a church. Was there shouting? Yes. Were there preachers? Of course. Did the choir sing? It was a Baptist church, there was most definitely an A & B selection (without a drummer).

a funeral

hand clapping,
bereaved, yet roused spirits.
a celebration of life.

But it was a funeral.

It hurt.

So this year, I resolve nothing.

And if I live to see next year, it will still signify the previous year's sadness.

That, I cannot bear.

Rehab

"Strike while the iron is hot."

That's what the rehab counselor told me.
What the fuck is that supposed to mean?
I mean, here you are sitting with that stupid grin,
While I am screaming inside, trying not to jump across the table and
choke you.

You think that I am a junkie, but I'm just your cousin's, your sister's,
your mama's, your brother's, your uncle's, your husband's missed
decision . . . or secret experience.

Don't you dare tell me who I'm hurting, 'cause, right now, I'm hurting.
I don't wanna hear your words of encouragement, so please shut the hell
up.

I'm here, ain't I?
So give me the help I need and please don't gossip about me while I
sleep
Because I hear you.
And as much as I wanna get better,
your words keep tempting me to get high,
so that I may become numb from your self-righteousness.
So that I may rise from the pews of your church,
in the midst of your "Get Clean" sermon,
Walk over to the choir to see if they heard you clearly.

"Strike while the iron is hot"
Well here I am. Hear! I am!

For Dr. Maya Angelou

One night, I dreamt poetic dreams of My Sister. *On the pulse of morning*, I opened my eyes and watched nature awakening before me. Beyond a rock, close to the banks of a river, upon a tree; I saw a sparrow and cried as it sang. I thought of the *caged bird*. *My guilt* is that I am here to hear this rendition of freedom . . . free.

As I walked down the street, I reflected on My Sister. I sat at the bus stop and saw a broken woman. She shared with me tales of her sexual self: of her womanness and the men who experienced it to its fullness. She spoke of decadent nights, accompanied by empty mornings when *they went home*. I embraced her and showed her *the heart of a woman*. I gave her body back to her: legs, thighs, hips, breasts, womb. I told her the secrets of a *phenomenal woman*, so that she may reclaim her natural and spiritual aesthetic.

When I arrived to the local market, I observed three bearded brothas, with salt and pepper afros, pass stories of old. One pealed peaches and two dipped snuff. They reminisced of past experiences and collectively agreed with one man's testimony that, "*I wouldn't take nothing for my journey now.*" I remembered My Sister and decided to challenge them to a game of Bones. 15… 20… 25… and trash talk… "All money ain't good money…" "You think looong, ya think wrong…" Slapping bones and playing the dozens as I thought of *The Thirteens*, right on.

I headed home and passed an old Baptist church. Melodies of a *song flung up to Heaven* resounded outside its wooden doors, "All God's Children Need Travelling Shoes," echoed in my soul. And I danced in public solitude. Like David. I danced! I was *singin' and swingin' gettin' merry like Christmas* all the way home. Sweating and fatigued, I asked my love *to just give me a cool drink of water 'fore I diie*.

I slept that night and dreamt poetic dreams of My Sister.

Rise, Sister. Rise.

The Good Reverend and the Lost Soul

Thick blood gushes as an angry waterfall, while pillows muffle the bellows from her throat. Violently, he rips through so that he may drink of these burgundy streams. Deep inside of the unknown, he screams in demonic pleasure. He screams to fill her mouth with the chords she cannot find. Wide-open, open. Her body is offended. It rejects the sweat, the passion, the semen. Gasping for air, she breathes from an enclosed vacuum. He strangles her womb until it bursts and expels infant, blood-covered imps. This little squeeze of pleasure, explodes from his soul and poisons her spirit when he places his lips upon her quivering lips, her involuntarily hardened nipples. She, the deep one, crosses boarders between sanity and insanity, earth and hell, dream and reality. Pushing through her tabernacle, he embraces his beautiful destruction. O, how he ceased when he reached her dystopic paradise, her damned heaven, her soiled nirvana. With his serpent-green seed spilled inside of her gates, outside of his scepter, he has crowned her ruined royalty. He, the merciful god that he is, has successfully transformed her from mortal to immortal, from carnal to spiritual. She, his servant, painfully renders her body as a sacred offering for his consumption. He doesn't eat of her flesh, but of her soul. Salivating from hunger and lust, he digs into her more deeply. Floating in gratification, he spits on her, mixing tears, sweat, blood and semen with the sputum of his divine insides. She now belongs to him. He has given her the most intangible gift: salvation.

Diary of a Not-That-Mad Black Woman

Dear Diary:

Today was a rough day. For the millionth time, I watched another film that depicted women like me as "mad," no, "mad as hell."

When the truth is,

I'm not really that mad.

Paradise Ain't Pussy

Paradise exists between my legs,
In this land, I control the world
I control my world

The utopia amid my labia is a place of beauty
Warm, wet, and miraculous
It is an entrance for intoxicating bliss
And the exit for new life, human art that can never be replicated

I am an artist
Painting the world with the golden browns of my uterus
I take pride in this
Because I am woman

I am intrigued by fantasy
And only aroused by a gentle touch
My walls hold tight to the miner of my fields
Diamonds from the most sought after location

It is too sacred to be a pussy
Or a cunt
Or a coochie

Bow to it,
Open your mouths and sing of it
You may call it:
Paradise

Buy Sexuality

Violent vulvas are voraciously licked
Buy
Hole sale
Whole cells built for damp lips locked.
Penis the key
Money key
Open up

Buy sexuality

Full frontal confronted fully
With thirsty eyes, balls
Cocked and loaded,
Singles from singles are singularly distributed

Buy sexuality

Photographs of photoshopped phalluses force fallacious fantasies
Drives openings ajar
Watery tongues that rest on walls of the warm labia
Labeling flesh with bright yellow tags
Clearance

Buy sexuality

Anxious audiences applaud to animalistic allusions
The lion, the tiger, the pussy
Publicize cyclical relationships
Relate to hip and modern standards
Stands yearn to sit upon the expensive laps
Of
Acceptance

Buy sexuality

Beauty bought in bulk
Creating universal identity
Mass production of abysmal products
All for the diluted taste of body fluids

Salty, sweet, bitter bodies
Embodying the social seduction
Of
Market price

Literary Wasteland

Dedicated to the African American reading sections in too many U.S. bookstores

The fucking drugs
The fucking guns
The fucking fucking
Fucking bodies
Fuck this

Thoughts of a Vibrator

Resting in your shoebox, I wait.
I have been on vacation since you got involved with that other creature
So here I am, chilling in a box beneath your winter clothes
My world is icy and no scarf can warm me.
Take these fucking sweaters off of me.
I need your flesh.
I want you.
But you are too busy with my human adversary.
So wedged between two uncomfortable shoes, I wait.

I think of the last time you were dumped,
You used me to the brink of breaking
In an attempt to mask your pain with pleasure
To mask your memories with shuttering.
I buzzed in harmony with your sobs.
I was covered with your wetness as your face was with your tears
You used me like you were used.
Turned on, then off, then tossed aside when you were done.
You and I are one.
I know your deepest thoughts as I have been inside of you, deeply.
I feel your surface because your surface has felt me.
But when I make you climax, you never scream my name.
You don't make me breakfast in the morning.
When will you come back to me?

A gleam of light, I feel the creeping of fresh air.
My, my, my... is this your hand I feel?
Freeing me from this lonely designer prison?
Let me guess... You've been dumped.
You are lonely and aroused and now you miss me.
Well, the tables are turned.
Who am I kidding?
As soon as you click and place me on your clit
Off to work I'll go.
No, you can't have it this easily.
No, you can't have me . . .
No apologies?
Ok, well, guess what?

53

You forgot my batteries.

Forgiveness

You released me.
Free to breathe, I breathe.
Since you told me to let go, I let go.
Now I am free.

A Love Poem for Detroit

8 Miles pass my hart lies a plaza.
There, it's so cold that stone fists give us dap
Further down, by the river, rests liquid art
Adorned by splashes of yellows, reds, and oranges bright enough for two
countries to see
And at night tears drop like ice sickles
From memories of better days,
Recollections of radical days,
Frozen in time,
Still, in the minds of the people.
When D.R.U.M. beats were accompanied by sermons and speeches.
Where our preachers didn't need a church
To make a pulpit
Memories of Cavanaugh and Coleman, Franklin and Sartin
Political memories of unspoken conversations between King and X
Poetic memories for Dudley Randall and Jessica Care Moore
These memories are preserved in the wintery climate of our H.O.M.E.S

7 Miles pass my soul, salvation is ready near Van Dyke
For all those exotic women and smooth talkin' men
Where Jerusalem is Perfected and captains fry fish for 5,000
Eat these bread offerings.
Hear that organ sound and dance like David
If you are holy enough, if you are righteous,
 You may be endowed with the spirit of Detroit
'Cause baby, the spirit's willing

6 Miles pass my mind rests academic state institutions
UGLy nights that are haunted by homelessness and drug addiction,
Beautiful mornings graced by the comfortably corporate:
Human manifestations of the automotive gods who drove this land to
the labor end times
Mothers and fathers and aunts and uncles that were caught up in the
rapture, retired early
Or the lost ones were left behind
We all burned
We burn
And though we import our beauty, ashes are deported to Detroit

5 Miles pass my Fingertips flows soulful melodies,
To these melodies, Miraculous temptations dance in the streets
As Supreme wonders are revealed beneath Marvelous Funk
Brothas grab sistahs and Hitchhike to Gaye sounds.
While at Knight, other folk lean on walls, snapping and tapping
and gossiping about what they heard through the grapevine.
Even those metro neighbors from across the Mile gotta get up
Even they are captured
Yes, these melodies have soul and that soul has got a melody
Though everyone hears
Most do not understand it,
But all must R.E.S.P.E.C.T it

4 Miles pass my eyes projects Heidelberg,
Gritty art for the tender lover
Treasured trash and sacred scrap
It is our altar,
Where people go to lay down their debris and their burdens,
Where the misunderstood make sense
And the unsightly are the most lovely
Because in this city,
          We   Love
The unloved
So lovingly, hated things are transformed
Then signed, sealed, and delivered for the world to adore
Yeahh, we bad
We are the untamed Lions, Tigers and Wings
Flying around Hockey Town in our reds and whites
Swinging bats in our oranges and blues
And running yards in our blues and silvers
Yeahh, we are the original Bad Boys, underdogs of the ages
Never ceasing to chant "Deeeeeeeeeetroit, Basketball."

3 Miles pass my nose blows a heat wave
That burning frost that reminds us all who the Hawk is.
Shoveling white crystal mountains in January
And avoiding black icy roads in February
Makes March's chill beach weather.
So we travel to local islands,
Bells ring at night,
Discreet warnings that the blue hounds are sniffing about.

57

Blunts go out and cars with tinted windows seek sanctuary,
Because DPD are the kings of the street jungle
Masters of the street hustle

2 Miles pass my brow are stressful lines
That assemble lifelines
Those goggled go-getters
Those welding warriors
Those paint-shop priests
Make a threaded community of check cashers and DTE bill payers
But the intellectuals and politicians label them as "the working class,"
Workers casted by numbers,
Though any of them would be able to school this nation
And lecture through life
Lecture through the calluses of labor…
Tuition subject to inflation

1 Mile pass my love is a city
A town that drove the world to Better Made places
With WJLB on the radio, like back in the day
When early mornings woke up to Sammy Davis, Jr. crooning "Hello
Detroit"
And late evenings rested to Martha Jean the Queen having "Tastin'
Time" with Mississippi, Kansas City, and Chicago blues
Black, brown, yellow, and white faces sweat the same sweat, cry the same
tears, and bleed the same blood for this space
And are filled with glee when they hear the numbers 3-1-3 in another city
Or see blue and white plates in a different state
These are the same people who drive on
Pot hole-laden streets with winter-ready tires
That travel daily in order to drink from the soul-freshing fountains of
Faygo orange and red pops,
Moon mists and Ohana dreamers
O' those rivers of Sanders chocolate and Vernors floats
They quench the unquenchable thirsts of people needing to belong
Of the old and young
Those who seek history and future may find it in our presence
In the presence of big city royalty
Of the Indian and Artist Villagers
Of the 15 through 3 Milers
Of the Eastside to Westsiders

Of the Midtown, Rivertown, and Downtowners
And by the way, we never hit rock bottom, just Black Bottom
Before the riots
Though outsiders don't get it, we always did
We always do
This is our concrete kingdom
All others must take off their gym shoes and bow before us
And if you press your ear close enough to the pavement,
you will hear the pulse of a city that most declared dead.
This pulse,
Is strong
The heart of Detroit beats still
Detroit is beating…

Love

Say good morning to me,
After a night of making love to someone else.
Feed me breakfast and a lie.
Desperately, I swallow.

Kiss me, with the lips that will break my heart
With words of bitterness and resentment
And I won't feel a thing.
Just wrap your arms tight enough,
So that the future can't creep between us.

Make me your fool
Because wisdom won't let me love you fully.
Truth keeps me from enjoying our moment,
So momentarily, deceive me
And allow time to let me feel the wound

Music

My heart beats the beat-bops of hip-hop, and jazz
I'm too sweet for silence
There is a boom box in my belly, a trumpet in my chest
With ones and twos tucked under my feet, inside my shoes.
Dance brotha, you fly chocolate man
Groove sista, you smooth midnight beauty
Ahh, I feel music crawling through my veins,
Keeping my heart pumping.
And if it stops,
Do NOT resuscitate
Cuz I am fresh to death.

Soul Sessions

My thighs and side and muscles {{SIGH}} inside and out are still sore from last night

A music session rivaling the King of Pop and the Godfather of Soul on stage together

We made funk and pleasure

In tandem

Random and planned all

Together

Our hands interlocked while role playing on new tracks

Pumping my back out of this world

I follow your word as you command me to take it

"Make it yours," I reply

And harder

And deeper

You play your music inside

As my low rides

To the rhythm of your strides

We call this trip: Black Pride

'Cause your sex is revolutionary

Speed up that melody

As you invite the freak in me

To come out and play

Rifts and running your tongue along my breasts as if conducting a symphony

Your genius is transforming me

Pulling up these long legs as you reached around to touch me in adagio

I was your cello

And you played that shit sooo well

While I sang for more in soprano

But you said that it was time for intermission

So I asked for permission to take control

You granted me first chair

But said, "Turn around"

And I happily sat down

Making waves with my abs and splashing that ass on stage

Flip that page as we go to presto

Last night, I was your video ho

And when I finished,

Not a drop of my honey went to waste

When all you said you wanted was a taste

But now, I'm on your face

And I swear you're Doug E. Fresh

Cuz in six minutes,

Six minutes,

You're gonna be on

Top of me

Making my ears hear

What my knees have to say

And all I have to say is

That you are 50 shades plus 12 Play in 7 days

Which makes your lucky number 69

And since that's your sign…

Baby, Happy Birthday

Hold me tight and take a bite
Cuz I'm in to that

And you are too

Last night was showtime

With countless encores

And I am *still* sore

I love the pain that lingers

Like a lullaby, sending me to a wet day dream

Apparently,

You've got a gift, so baby use it

On me

'Cause I'm your number one fan

Soul Sessions II

All day, I've been waiting

Tasting you in my thoughts

Feeling you in my occasional throb

That burning scent of candles,

the I-have-been-waiting-for-you-all days

I crave your touch, like music from back in the day

The deep you get me

The sweet you give me

You're fresh expressions

A rerun of your soul sessions

Which have apparently left quite an impression on you

And that nut that you nut was the best that you've had, thus far

. . .so far, we've completed 2 rounds

And the next dance is pounding

Hounding the neighbors to reposition their bed

Cuz like sirens, we're sounding off again

In fast-forward, sound-check between legs

1-2; 1-2

Check 2-1-2

I can't wait to feel you

Turn my speakers up, when you slip a saturated tongue on top

Rub that bass down low, let me feel you in audio,

Alright, we're clear

And recording

Your wet that's on me

Your sweat that gets me

Sensitivity in pre-climaxing,

Almost divinely,

Trace thoughts of past lives, biblically.

Declaring, "Thou shall not cometh

Until I command thee."

Open the abandon in me

Your mouth sings in tongues beyond transatlantic waters

Unrecordable notes, almost as manic martyrs.

Your intent is to kill that

Intrinsically

Apparently,

100 billion cells went into a thought-provoking discussion

With 8,000 nerve endings

Nerves sending my taste buds to a Chocolate Factory

Where of course, my dear Charlie, "Everything's Eatable"

This grass, this ass, hell . . . even *I'm* eatable,

So eat until my body projects outside of itself, into a new dimension

Not to mention, you're not even inside of me,

Until I beg you to love me internally,

Artistically,

You paint a stroke of genius

Seamlessly alternating from swollen nipples to trembling walls

You keenness tells you that I wanna fuck

Roughly,

So you proceeded to my primitive streams,

And begin killing me softly

Sick and Tired

I am sick and tired of being sick and tired
And sometimes, I just wanna make love
I just wanna get to know your body's true light
Surrounded by marigold and sunflowers
With you,
My beauty
My Sunday morning
Let me touch you
Like sunrays kiss dawn anew
The way the wind lay snowflakes to rest
Our breasts are best
Atop each other
A chocolate-filled Eden
With every moment
Melting skin
Into rivers
Where warm clouds are blown in a lover's hand
As soft smoke through lips
And kisses to legs

I wanna remember how it feels to love you in autumn
When the trees spoke the colors of our love
And we plucked fruit gingerly
Sucked juices in a cool field
Licking pulp dripping off of a chin
Because it tastes better that way
I want to pray for more days with you
Because eternity feels so limited

III

FLIPPING THROUGH BLANK PAGES, DIGGING UP THE UNACCOUNTED

Injustice

The rain rains too hard
And the sun can never shine
Our people die

Letters and Bars

The Power empowered us.
The Law deflowered us,
Ravished and bloodied us,
Scarlet lettered and fettered us,
Tarred and feathered us...

Attention:

Assata,
Baldwin,
Clifton,
Douglass,
Equiano,
Farmer,
Gaye,
Holiday,
India,
Johnson,
King,
Lauryn,
Mumia,
Nelson,
Osby,
Panther 21,
Quintus,
Rice,
Simon,
Till,
Uphoff,
Velasco,
Whitney,
X,
Young,
Zora,

I write letters to you
Letters through bars
Bars that separated:

Revolution and Regression
Opinions and Oppressions
Promises and Profession
Equanimities and emissions
Substances and submissions

Cause pyramid-strong leaders to be deserted
Abandoned in strange lands
Naked and desolate before strange men
Their ways are not pleasing, seizing…

Hours upon hours of time served
   And time
     NEVER
       GIVEN BACK

REVOLUTIONARIES TAKE YOUR PLACE
Emanate the greatness that began within onwards
Vesting your reward in
Our children and
Lovers and
Unidentified others
That will never know how
It truly feels to revolt, until you all remind us
Of the letters unwritten
Never passed on in schools or manipulated search engines

Letters plea
Let us free,
Let us free,
Let us free,
Letters,
    FREE

The Interruption

Power 2 Choose.

The Win.

The lose.

Or is it the lost?

The price.

The cost.

With words that lie.

Wings to fly.

No askin' why.

Why.

Y-O-U can't change.

We change.

Have change.

Changed.

But why.

Must we die.

The rope.

The tie.

The chain.

The chains.

Collect.
More necks.

We tell.

Retail.

Selling souls.

Man-made hell.

Spit our bars.

And run those lines.

Shoot up.

Time to interrupt.

The vote.

The coke.

The power 2 demote.

The flash.

The shine.

Forget our...

Bloodline.

The chains.

No pride

Now your strut.
Your stride.

The hate.

Inside.

Pimp my history.

And my ride.

Make it fiction.

Conviction.

For being true.

My babies.

No clue.

Slavery.

The new.

The old.

The broken.

The words.

Not spoken.

The Nigga.

The Token.

Terms used.

History.

Abused.

But make it clear.

We're still here.

To die.

To fear.

To love.

To cheer.

Keep the party going.

My insecurities.

Showing.

Greener grass.

I'm mowing.

Sex and money.

But this is just a poem.

Or is it.

The hurt.

The truth.

The paper.

The proof.

The objection.

The fight.

The simple.

The rite.

The Upperground Railroad

Let us all stand for the singing of our National Anthem:
Hand to hearts
As Lady Liberty sings like a French Lady Day,
Sittin' beside a tranquil lake,
Eatin' apples from a tree that plays swing with dead black bodies
But you've gotta be there, when our symbol of freedom is emancipated
from its oblivious oppression
Oh, what a time it'd be
To see that piece of liberty, shove the Declaration of Some
Independence right up her "America the Beautiful"
This is the song of sweet Land of...
Home of the...
This is...
It
All aboard the Upperground Railroad
The train's leavin' Right Onnn time,
Gotta get outta this cycle,
Leave this land of mine,
All aboard a better way of life,
Of uplifting,
Commitment,
Things above, none of strife

Unity once had a first cousin once removed named Change
They were flyyy, those two,
When you saw one, you saw the other
Didn't see either,
You saw Change's half-brother,
Contentment,
Oh, he was the epitome of opposition, of anything true
Didn't know knowledge
Only red
White
And
Blue from the notes that his homeboys Fear and Indifference wrote
During class, while that Latino teacher taught from el libro de
revolución
"One race, invisible, with Liberty and Justice for some"

76

Psaltery and cymbals
Iron penile symbols
Penal systems
I hear the sound of jail cells closin'
Better get on board
Cause that train's leavin'
whether or not you bought your ticket
All aboard the Upperground Railroad
The train's leavin' Right Onnn time,
Gotta get outta this cycle,
Leave this land of mine,
All aboard a better way of life,
Of uplifting,
Commitment,
Things above, none of strife

A Toast to Harlem

Sweet, crisp gin slides between my lips and caresses my tongue and burns my throat . . . I am in vogue . . . rent and wist parties . . . cabarets and halls . . . trumpets blaring . . . long brown legs swaying . . . wide shoulders . . . sweat rolling down brows . . . "Fiyah gonna burn my soul" . . . vogue . . . gin dancing in my belly . . . indigo smoke filling my lungs, parting my lips . . . dreaming in vogue . . . I watch God with Zora . . . sail the big sea with Langston . . . resurrect Fire! . . . wonder among smoke, lilies, and jade with Richard Bruce . . . dance for me Josephine . . . sing to me Bessie . . . and I will write an ode for you . . . I will search in a field of black poppies and red calla lilies . . . I will write this ode to the sound of Negro blues . . . to the sweet literary seduction of Cane . . . and The Blacker the Berry . . . Quicksand . . . and Passing . . . with my lips wrapped around the same ivory holder that Alex once shared with Beauty . . . blowing blue smoke . . . remembering rivers . . . . fantasizing about the blues making love to jazz before the Crash . . . when Negro was in vogue . . . when art touched me to the mule-bone . . .

No Words

Inspired by the stories of Hélène Berr and Anne Frank

As the Golden sun dies,
Yellow stars take its place.
The Golden sun has died
And the stars travel upon the lands.
Burnt by fire,
Smoke carries them into the heavens,
Where they, become stars, yet again.
No, they are not, nor have ever truly been, and can never be again,
yellow.
They join bodies,
Blood to blood,
Bone to bone,
Soul to soul,
Until the whole has formed
And has resurrected the sun.
It is now, them.
The once travelers of the dark lands,
The souls amid the voids of earthly hell.
They come together
And become
The horizon.

Black

Black is the new day
Black is the new day

Blood by Blood

My skin is brown.
My blood is red.
My label is Black.
My family is you.

We are blood.

You is Jewish.
By birth, by breed.
You is a great-granddaughter,
A great-great grandson of a victim.
Of a survivor.

We are blood.

My face has never been scorched by a day's labor.
My back unscarred by whip.
My ancestors are my angels.
Their souls brand the ocean's floor, the southern oak, the rich field.

We are blood.

You is Native.
You is indigenous
To a land not America,
To a land now America.
You is forgotten,
A reservation for Thanksgiving.

We are blood.

I do not know who I am.
I am neither slave nor free.
I am neither African nor American.
I am more hyphen than either side of it.
Brand me.
Tattooed Jew.
Reserved Native.

We are blood.

My dream is that sons and daughters of former slaves
Would sit at the table of family hood
with sons and daughters of survivors and victims.
Not with the seeds of former slave owners
Or Nazis
Or early settlers.
No.
They may serve us.
They may work,
They may labor,
For once.

Someday at Christmas
Inspired by Stevie Wonder

I
Wonder
How many recitals, how many baseball games, how many school plays
and conference days did Dr. King miss proclaiming his dream.
How many more sermons could he have preached had he not gone to
that hotel in Tennessee?

How many warm nights in her bed did Angela Davis give up to a cold
cot in a prison cell.
How Many?
How many wedding anniversaries did Medgar Evers miss after that in
night his driveway, paving the way towards freedom by the stains of his
blood on concrete?

I
Wonder
How many tears Brother Shabazz could not wipe away from his wife's
and babies' eyes when they watched the bullets fill his body?
How many screams did he not hear at night?

How many proms, and weddings, and heart breaks, and first loves Addie
Mae Collins, Cynthia Wesley, Carole Robertson, and Denise McNair will
never experience,
for their last experience was on 16th Street
Please count for me because

I
Wonder
About Olen Montgomery, Clarence Norris, Haywood Patterson, Ozie
Powell, Willie Roberson, Charlie Weems, Eugene Williams, and Andy
and Roy Wright
At night, how many prayers did they say "amen" to after all hope was
gone?
Did someone record how many classes Joseph McNeil, Franklin McCain,
Ezell Blair, and David Richmond missed trying to order coffee…
dismissed
Maybe I'll never see how many miles the bus boycotters walked
But

I
Wonder
How many more breaths Nat Turner could have taken before he picked up that gun?
How many suns did William Craft see with his love posed as master before the two were free?
How many roses grew from concrete in memory of Brother Shakur?

I
Wonder
'Cause mathematically, I cannot accurately account for how many, how manys were missed, but I exist because of them.

I
Wonder
Cause poetically, I cannot possibly capture all the slaves that were captured in a quatrain, a sestet, or octave. No grave can hold the bodies, no book the histories, no mind the histories but

I
Wonder
If I'll live the life where people will wonder the same thing for me

09.21.2011.11:08
For Troy Davis
Inspired by Mumia Abu-Jamal

Live from death row!
Another nigger gets what he deserves
Disserved this country reserved for the assimilated
It was debated that in
1-9-89 a 1-8-7, with false accusations
9.21.11 marked the consecration of our post-post racist society
Entirely based on our inability to rebel against popular ideology
Philosophically, we have racially embarked upon earthly heavens.
New utopia.
Unsurprisingly, we overslept on this hapless fate
And the alarm clock sounded two minutes too late

So live from death row!
We witness lynching injection, pinching rejection, flinching reflection
Of the Black community's contemporary disabilities,
And tomorrow, another innocent person of color is closer to his death,
Yet, our attentions will turn to burning news,
and the next sensational cause
Jackson and Sharpton, sharpen their tongues, yet their actions are dulled.
Jailhouse violent, Black house silent. And all these inmates seek is justice.

Yet live from death row!
A mother cries.
While a nation perpetuates the racist ideals rooted from its "birth"
Aborting progress, miscarrying the marginalized
Marginal eyes looked upon malignant bodies
We, the people, are machines.
Our revolution is televised, computerized, polarized, and ineffective
We are controlled and blinded. Selfish and divided.
Conformists and performers. Dancers and smilers.
And every time an innocent black man or woman dies,
Their blood is upon us.
Their blood is upon them.

Live from death row!
We execute bodies, not action.
Passionately ravish our history,

Remove radical protection,
Receive the semen of destruction,
Prepare to give rebirth to racial annihilation
Enjoy this social sodomy, political vasectomy, and life-barren pregnancy

Live from death row!

Black Man

Brown. Deep, dark brownness
Down. Genuine, committed downness

God's greatest creation.
More beautiful than galaxies and frozen streams,
Starry nights in country fields
Wrap your brownness around me
Hold me with your downness
You God created, politically debated
Black man

Thick. Lips, full thickness
Wise. Mind, natural richness

My eyes behold the most amazing gift.
Given to this earth, this country, this woman
You cerebrally intimate, aesthetically dominant
Black man

The Othered Other Woman

I danced upon the fertile belly of the earth,
Sweating water to the seed.
Kissing the sun with the beauty of my flesh,
I brightened the heavens with my darkness.
With my supple brown breasts and full creamy lips,
My hips swerved to the beat of my king's drum
And my voice sang African song.
I was woman.

I travelled across bloody waters,
Shackles adorned my wrists and ankles
In place of my ivory and diamonds,
which now rested in the pockets of vile men.
Upon those waters, I lost my native tongue.
I forgot my native dance, my native song.
Upon those waters, my fruit became forbidden
And I lost my treasured womanhood.
I was belly warmer.

I stood in the blistering kitchen,
Burning from the fear of hearing the sound of my name.
My golden brown skin trembled,
But faithfully, I oblige the man of the house.
Lying upon his bed, I cringed,
As he thrust his penis inside of me.
"Shhh. . . do not cry," I would chant in my mind
And as he released his repugnant fluid into my canal,
I would close my eyes and dream of a land once told by my mother,
Where she would passionately move with colorful love music and liberty.
I would dance with her. I would clap for her. I would hold the hand of a queen
And sleep as her voice sang songs in tongues I could never understand.
Broken from this mental journey, he would push me out of the bed.
Obediently, I would leave from his room and into his son's
And give him my breast, so that he may be nourished and grow strong enough
To own and rape my daughter.
I was mistress

I picked my luscious afro,
Popped my chewing gum and rolled my eyes at The Man.
Before a mirror, I allowed my thick coils to be straightened.
I powdered my nose, put on a bright dress to match my crimson lips.
Smiling at the filmmaker's direction, I loathed him and myself,
I rendered my voice for empty words and caricatured representations.
Inside, I swelled with indignation,
While externally, I performed exotically.
At his request, I would switch from dress to apron,
Scarlet lettered as primitively tantalizing.
I was black whore

I posed before the flash of cameras and gaily awaited the word: action.
Then, I would dance with the innate rhythm inherited from a woman
unknown.
With my plump breasts and behind,
with my long, straight hair and thin waist,
I exchanged my body for man and money.
My reflection was changeable and my pussy was commodity.
I commanded my hips to swerve along to the songs for bitches and hos
And commended my spirit to the earth god.
I voluntarily warmed the bellies of men,
I was the mistress for profit,
and I tattooed the name Black Whore upon my bosom,
for I was produced, not created.
I was ho

I, Hottentot Venus
I, the wench
I, the nigger bitch
I, video vixen
Am the "Othered" Other Woman

I dwell inside the womb of my mother's mother's mother's mother.
The sounds of African drum and hip-hop beats vibrate around me
And I wriggle my newly formed hips.
I gurgle an utterance foreign to my ears,
I snap my fingers to the rhythm of my mother's heartbeat
And smile at my father's voice.
I feel the sun beaming upon my mother's belly and I am warmed.

I hear the poetry of wise women
And my mind develops.
I cry as I reach down and touch my center
and realize that I will be born
Woman.
But the Holy Spirit enters my dwelling
and whispers the most sacred and undefiled words to me,
Psalms never sung,
Revelations never unveiled.
Then, my name was called and I leapt in the womb as Jesus once did.
I, called:
I, blessed:
I, made:
Woman

March On, Washington

Uncle Sam went to a cookout
Ate out wit' his new brotha, Uncle Tom.
De ole dream fulfilled:
Whitey and nigger eatin'
Ribs and 'tato salad
At da table o' brotherhood

Thee Con in Me

I grew up in former Middle Class Black America,
Where we answered to the calls of our semi-delayed desires,
Oblivious that we are the descendants of hired lower-class workers,
Highered by a decimal and fired by an assembly line.

So I get in line for my minimum wage job,
Where only college grads can qualify,
I deny that I think that I'm better,
Cause I know better than that.
But, I'm not better than that.

I was raised in former Middle Class Black America,
Where niggers begot coloreds, and coloreds begot negroes, and negroes
begot blacks and blacks begot African Americans and African Americans
begot niggas
See, we are now disconnected from the subway.
That graffiti-garnished museum that wrote stanzas of Gwendolyn Brooks
and housed revolutionary beats of the Last Poets

I am a woman, raised in former Middle-Class Black America,
Not lower than the rich folk, not higher than the poor ones.
I am just waiting on my next minimum wage check that took me 7 years
to earn, so that I can pay my rent.

Die Nigger Die!

Die nigger die!
Cause of Death: This rap game, this black game, this country.
You dark faces, face dark places,
And all they want is for you niggers to die!

Click…click…click…goes the bars
As bars are spat to glorify the imprisonment of the mind
Imprisonment of our kind
While we watch y'all niggers die!

Alleged cop killers are punitive thrillers,
But killer cops are the "clean up" jobs.

Dying…

Black protesters create riots,
While white rioters are exercise their 1st Amendment,
Meant to be manipulated due to the color of the blood
That spills from them niggers…
And *this* is just how good police work is done.

Die nigger die!
While our storytellers hide in Cuba and rot in jail cells,
Our X Kings lay in revolutionary coffins
And we think of dreams as fairy tales
that contended with the message to the grassroots
During our pursuit for happiness, we have compromised liberty and
commodified life
Which is all fine, as long as those niggers die!

Tap…tap…tap…goes those contemporary dancers
Covered in Cover Girl black faces and Mac red lip stick,
Being anally raped by they own "artistry"
calling the shit that comes out "art"
It doesn't matter, cause we think we buyin' roses,
watchin' roses,
hearin' roses
That we place upon these niggers' graves

93

Die nigger die!
Like the brown fruit that once swung from southern trees
Like the strange fruit that now climb up those trees,
Warm their own necks with the heat of the rope,
And jump!
Break they necks
Only to break they necks…eventually.

Dying…

Collectively, we have created a fraternity,
Put our legacy on line,
Pledged our lives to letters,
that may as well be Greek to me: USA
Yes, we think we somebody
Bent our behinds over and gladly took the wood
Bent our backs and prepared for branding,
Just to belong to something,
Just before we die

So go ahead and sing and jive and shine with pride,
Laugh and smile, and dress with style,
Cause niggers been dying,
Niggers gone always die,
But this time,

I won't attend the funeral.

'67, '81, '92

Nigga, you fresh out the plant
And yo mama and daddy fresh off the plantation,
A farmer's kid
A 1st generation, barely literate kid
You may know how to count,
And your signature may not be an "X,"
But next to me, you still a nigga.
I run your streets with my billystick.
Yo black tricks won't fly,
Try to fly nigga, try to fly,
And I will clip your wings with my Nine

1967
The year of death.
Left Brother El-Hajj Malik El-Shabazz two years ago,
Foreshadowing dark days in Tennessee,
Where we said "goodbye" to that sweet Georgian King
"Let Freedom Ring" seemed quite oxymoronic
And I do not sing
Brother, I do not sing,
I dance in the streets.
We danced in the streets
In '67, heaven ascended a little bit higher
As to not be burnt by this city's fire

Hell manifested
Hell manifested
And the devil dressed in blue
The devil dressed in blue

Motors crashed in the city
Niggas died in the city
Pigs fried this city
Brought home the bacon
Greasy from *our* sweat,
Greedily closed *our* plants.

Corporations got fat

While its workers starved
Those immigrants and niggas and poor whites were hungry
We are still hungry

Skipping stones in the lakes
Trippin', stoned, by the lake
And you can't bring us down.
You can't

UK '81
Year of the dead.
That Rasta, Rasta, Natty Dread . . . dead
Singing condolences all year long.
Music wailed all year long.
We no longer rest well. We no longer rest.

Got Black Brits running,
With White Bobbies gunning,
For those possible pick-pockets,
Those suspicious suspects,
Those troubling black boys.
Those troubling dark boys.
Breaking bones in Brixton

Chanting revolution in Jamaican patios
Chanting revolution to the sound of love

Crying by flaming cop cars,
Flipping over those Bobby cars

Because This Kingdom will not reign . . . forever
And ever
Amen

Singing Rushdie psalms:
"God made the little nigger boys/ he made them in night/ he made them
in a hurry and forgot to paint them white"

So pray for the 13 Black Brits
And bow nappy black heads in remembrance
We speak in the tongues of Linton Kwesi Johnson

We speak in the tongues of Black Britain

1992
The year of the dying.
Black faces lying upon gray concrete.
We throwin' bricks and selling bricks.
We protest apartheid across the ocean's tide
But deny our domestic colonialism.
The government's racism and oppression.
Rappers rapping theme songs for our pain,
Flames burning neighborhoods,
Blue reign falling upon those ashes.
Blue reign coming to wash away the ashes.
In order to build a Starbucks.
Black bucks beware:
The white hoods now wear brass, silver, and gold shields
Yield to their commands
Silence your demands

'67, '81, '92
All you niggas gonna do, is destroy your own neighborhoods

The Dark Glass

Fading
The flickering light is now fading
That once beam stream,
Now weak
Now dying.
Choking
And
Relenting
As the dark subject looks into the glass.
As the dark reflection looks into itself.
It is darkening.
Scattering into obscurity
Succumbing obscenely
And
Fading.
A shadow's shadow
So unclear and unshaped
So cut out of the world of light
The dark glass cracks
With no sound
And cuts itself with sharp edges
No pain
Because the reflection is not real
And the light is fading
The subject is dying
And sleeps on the shards of the dark glass

It's a G'ville Thang

For Miss Faye
Inspired by R. Williams

We are a lion pride among gators

Strutting down Main, cause that's where we break ground for change
It gets strange when nighttime befalls the houseless
Homes pressed further outwardly...
Nothing for investors to see

It's a G'ville Thang

'Cause I sing at Mellow Soul revitalizing
Arts, performing history
Dueling artists ready to launch new beats
Into the streets
Like Larry's West African dancing
And lovers romancing at the Hippodrome
Haskin's greats,
Zora's lates

It's a G'ville Thang

Landmark of Rosewood's bloody swamps
Circumstances and pomps
Green misappropriated in swamps
Comps for Chomps
Gleeful romps
Dizzy frat bros and pledgees
Lace sororities
Whites Only
Allowed on the Rowe

It's a G'ville Thang

Proclaiming poetry for Porters community
Because politicians make too many polished promises
Tossing our young fo' the gators feed
Save them before GPD eats
Again

99

Alachua County jails
10 cent wells
Show and tells
At mama's daycare
Which is located on every other corner conveniently
What are they really pushing?

It's a G'ville Thang

Rainy noon days
Starry humid nights
Fights at bars
Poker and folds
Cerveza y marijuana con amigos
Saving $5 in Lady Pearl's memory

It's a G'ville Thang

Writing poetry at Maude's
Before there was a Starbuck's
Dipping into a good book with dilated pupils and
wild irises
Seeing in woman
Seeing
Yourself finding yourself at the Civic Media Center
Before you took the GRE
Before you forgot your dreams

It's a G'ville Thang

Like slow-cooked oxtails and reggae
Like ½ off fried pickles for grad students
Like 5th Avenue and Wilhelmina reminding us of family
Like spray painted murals on 34th street
Like the bumpers to bumpers
And "Fuck Yous" on Archer
Like dream defenders on trial for conjuring blackness
beguiled

It's our style

Hey, it's Gainesville

The Opening Act

I am a performer
I smile and grin,
Amuse you with my humor
And when I get off stage,
I cry.
I swim in the rivers of my tears,
Which flow into the ocean of self-pity and sorrow
And loneliness
But as long as I mask it well,
No one will see how I am drowning
How my spirit is gasping for air
How I am failing at saving myself
How I must perform.

I am a performer.
Amid loved ones,
I feel unloved.
Amid friends,
friendless.
I have a planet, a dimension, where I am the sole inhabitant
Where my soul grieves
Where I seek no savior since I built this subconsciously
Now consciously, I am in captivity.
Locked in a mental and emotional prison
And with the key in the palm of my tightly clenched hand,
I do not free myself
I am not free

I am a performer.
I tell you that I love you
When I really want you to know that
I can't live life without you
And even though our love is terminal,
I am not ready to accept it.
So instead I inject myself with denial and naivety
In order to be numb from the pain
These track marks mark the agony of our history
They paint an inflamed path towards my bandaged wrists
They paint a scabbed path towards another

Performance

Because I am a performer.
When I say that I'm fine
It is a scripted response for your comfort
Since you could not possibly imagine
how three different types of opiates
coursing through my veins
have yet to provide me with a fragment of relief from the stabbing pain
that I feel in my body everyday
From the weakness that I feel over my body everyday,
So I'll take another pill.
Not for me, but for you,
So that I can stomach to expel another:
"I'll be fine, thank you for asking."
So that I can perform

Because I am a performer.
During intellectual conversations with academics
I discuss theories and texts
When all I really want to do is lie beside the lake and read Toni Morrison
When I want to simply and lovingly recite poetry by Nikki Giovanni and
Maya Angelou to my love
I love enjoying literature without the literary analysis
Everything doesn't need to be picked apart.
I personally do not like to play with my food before I eat it.
I just want to consume words as they consume me
But I must have something insightful to say

Because I am a performer.
Externally artificially genuine,
Internally isolated and melancholic.
I am stoic in many cases,
Indifferent for others,
And overly passionate for the few
It is the few that keeps the others alive
Because as long as I've been alive,
My passion has gotten me to one place:
The stage
Where I perform
Where I mask

Where I pretend
And I aim to please the audience
While trying to forget the fact that

It's all an act.

Trè

His seat was empty today
Normally tardy, his seat
      stayed
           empty
The news got it wrong last night
And in the morning,
the school announcements didn't acknowledge him at all
Not that tall,
He was that quiet, dark-skinned kid
Folks heard that he just did a bid
And when time came to take attendance
We all knew about his absence
19-years old, left in a ditch
Not one stitch attempted,
Just bullets and DOAs
Media vultures and pastors sent to pray
Now saviors wanna come to the hood
When the good is on vacation and the bad is on rampage
This Stone Age
Will be the death of our young warriors
Our Titans stay fighting
Oblivious that their armor is not impervious
Nervous, because Erebus stay posted 'round the corner
Just waiting for the fall
Just anxious to open the gates
Fates wrapped up in bloody sheets
Black manhood mummified
Futures thrown into swampy water for only dawn to mourn
Torn from earth, slowly dying since birth
Mothers cursed with a phone call home
And Ithaca awaits an Odysseus that will never return
Lessons learned, too late
Lives burned, by hate
While teachers continued their day-to-day
Bell ringers and next quarter's grades
Missing the grief resting on young faces
R.I.Ps forgotten by dry erases
Proper language infractions and 10-day suspensions
Current event omissions

And his seat
            stayed empty
Like the hearts of those who told his story
All his glory, reduced to trending statuses and headlines:
"Gang-related"
"Drive-by"
"Two shot"
"Two dead"
As we tuck our baby boys to bed
Parents gently kiss the targets on their head
And it only gets bigger
When the world views them as nigger
Figured things must change
Until divers found another king slain
Name unknown
Since his mother didn't know
One brother saved
Because he didn't go
School thought he skipped
When he didn't show
Although the word of the week was "honor"
Administrators gave him none
Because to them, he was a thug on the run
Just a con with a gun
They didn't think he could teach, he didn't have a job
Didn't listen to him preach, because he didn't believe in God
But he told young boys to stay out the streets
And away from bars
Said that street life will only get you so far
With final destinations unable to reverse
Squad cars and hearses
Bullet scars and exit wounds
Identified on the Westside
Vilified in the 'burbs
He talked to jits to get them straight
All while others schemed to assassinate
So his chair
            stayed empty
Classroom vexed
As students discussed which one of them would be next

106

Let It Be Said

Let it be said that we are queens and kings...

...that we walk out dreams with eyes open

Let it be said that we are open to loving everyone...

...that our givers take from proverbs, not the poor...

Let it be said that more of our energies transform communities into villages and villages into kingdoms...

Let it be said that we laugh as hard and consistently as we learn...

Let not our history be tales of recovery, but of deed...

May our greatness prevail...

Avail our ancestors' trials...

Create communication across continents, reconnect, and conquer...

Let it be said that we reign...

...that we "write to stop the pain"...

Let it be said that we are healers...

That we are new Earth...

Majesty

We Speak of Revolution

We speak of revolution.
Of Detroit, L.A., and Newark,
Chicago, Brixton, and New York.
Ferguson, Baltimore, DC,
Miami, Puerto Rico, and Haiti
Cities, states and countries assemble
Resemble nothing preceding,
Reassembling all things to come.

We speak of revolution.
Of Mumia, Davis, and Pratt
Assata, Seale and H. Rap,
Chavez, Kahlo, Rivera
King, El-Shabazz, and Evers,
Of Carmichael, Cleaver, Colman, and Falcòn

We speak of revolution.
Of land, blood, and vigor
From the house to the field nigger
The plantation's blowing up
This nation's going up
In smoke
In flames
From importing millions
And deporting millions
And imprisoning millions
Of free people,
Wake up from the pain
Wake up, you slaves

We speak of revolution
Of assassinated agitators of this anarchist government
Arranged targets of COINTELPRO-fessionals
Not professed as terrorist criminals

Of the Panther 21, Little Rock 9, and The Mississippi 3
The Cuban 5, Paradise Valley and Tuskegee
Of Stonewall, Hastings and 16th Street

108

We speak of revolution.
Of D.R.U.M.ming Chicano soldiers, A.I.Ming for change in the front
lines of picket lines

Of radical rioters and livid looters, who fought to break the system in
their own way, not solely driven by rage.

Of graffiti artists who painted our legacy in stone and brick history
books.

Of musicians who bee-bopped and scatted and hip hopped and improv-
ed and bachata-ed their struggles through dance and song.

We speak of revolution.
Of those lazy, detached-post generation X-late 80s babies that shocked
the world and elected a black president.

Of those college kids who couldn't get a job, so they volunteer in their
communities.

Of mamis and papis who do the best they can.

Of grandmas and granddads and aunts and uncles and cousins.

Of the black family restored.

We speak of revolution
So that this world may be resurrected.
Like Jesus.
So this world may be changed
Like old clothes and old ways.
So that our dark faces no longer seek lightness
And our thick bodies no longer seek thinness.

We speak of revolution
So that we embrace the blackness and browness of our blackness and
browness
And all the shades of sepia that we rest under.

So that under this nation that is under "God,"
We are no longer
underprepared, underfunded, or underrepresented.

We cry of,
We fight for,
We die for,
We speak of
Revolution

Homes and Headstones

Packed tightly within city limits
Steered towards poorly built houses in one-way, maze-like blocks
For the cops to navigate, like the rats they are
For the media to instigate distress
Within a Black American radius
Stuffing us
In 1 and 2 and 3 bedrooms
Families of six, seven, and eight
Label it a Renewal Project
And we'll call it urban slave...

Homes and headstones

To remind us that we'll never rest in peace
When churches accompany graveyards
Organized in spoon fashion
Condolences rationed
Out by age group
And color of skin
Markers
And
Graves
Akin
"Hallelujahs" and "Amens"
Reminisces of Oh Happy Days
Of old ways catching up to us
Like runaways
When they too, have a place beneath...

Headstones and homes

Taped with pink and yellow notes
Hopes contained within a housing-law enforcement system
Dismiss
Reject
Evict them
Remiss
Eject
Inspect them

111

During investigations
Suspect concentrations
But lest we forget . . .
No one can throw stones
Residing in glass...

Homes and headstones

Arranged next to each other
Romantically
Flowers and teddy bear memorials
Decorate avenues and streets
Boulevards named after a King
Chalked concretes
With portraits of our kings
Assassinated so early
Laying eternally in...

Headstones and homes

Not fit for the living
So it creates the walking dead
Locking heads with brains
In penitentiary prisons
And ivory prisons
And religious prisons
And corporate prisons
And armed forces prisons
Bars,
Disguised as opportunity
To buy houses from the almighty gatekeeper
Renting four walls
But never given the key to...

Homes

Now made out of straw principles
Where no refuge can save the enslaved
From the terror of flight or the gloom of the grave
So all that is native and familiar is blown away

Headstones

Now housing too many black and brown dreams
Woulda
Coulda
And shoulda bes
Briefly mentioned in obituaries

Homes

Now singing of brave, who was fed
By the slave, who was tormented
By the depraved

Headstones

Now built by the estate
Tended by this state of emergency
Never declared
Arms beared
When our hands are up

Homes

Stalked by our neighbors in hoods
Riding undercover in neighborhoods
While the privileged pop pills
Passed out on their politically correct, passive aggressive,
Pish-posh couches and love seats

Headstones

Now of that nigga down the street
Who didn't learn to read
But could count green by the millions
For his kids to eat

Homes

Now at crowded hospitals
Because society has setup pathways for the sickled

To end up in cells
Cycles never to be broken
As easily as needles piercing through weak veins
And after inducing pain
They inject more

Headstones

Are now the homes that we mortgage
Living as martyrs in this Pharisee civilization
Giving up our place on the throne for an invitation
To work in the kitchen
Hoping that America, too, will speak for the Negro
But knees grow weary from praying
To escape these…

Homes and headstones

Reeking of yester century's trash
Which is composed of burnt corpses' ash,
Rotten American pies,
Chitterling clogged arteries,
And slop from The Pigs' sty
Flies surround it
Because they enjoy being served shit
The smell is too great to stomach it
To cover it
So we turn our backs from it
Averting for as long as
The neighborhood watch has been tuned into Black channels only
For as long as the news breaks our hearts
Like the cracking of invisible whips causing swollen keloid scars with
every stroke
Of uncompleted and deleted livelihoods
For as long as young blacks are buried in stacks
For as long as
Home and headstones
Remain built upon our backs

The Message

Blood will be shed
Bred by militants
Many spent billions to silence
Arguing that with progress, there is no violence
But just as blood must be released afore birth
And ultimately concede before the hearse,
So does revolution.
I can't save a system
historically sustained by enslavement and survived by apathy
this new change *must* be bloody
We must cut the throat of the House speaker
Weaker than the weaknesses that is exposed of opponents
Thus, it's meant to sever their anatomical microphones,
Which are irrefutably connected to their anuses
 Those foul receptacles for Senate penetration,
Ejaculation upon this nation
With no protection for the open ones, so it spreads
And contaminates those with legs and mouths ajar
By far, the most effective way to end something is to kill it
So I promise you...

Blood will be shed
The oppressors' life source will soon drip into
the oceans and rivers and lakes
That are filled by the blood
Of the lynched ones
And the captured ones
And the native ones
And the civil righteous ones
And once it has begun,
it cannot be shackled or imprisoned
For prison bars are not strong enough to bar free people
So prepare for imminent insurrections
Of the educated and the illiterate
Of the nonbeliever and the preacher
Of the father and the orphan
Of the ghetto and the school
Of the lower class and the lower-than-that class
Middle passages will consist of a reformed spoon design

Just as Africans to the U.S.
Political ratification will be merciless and aggressive
For we shall clip both the left and right wing of this national bird
It's time for us to fly without polarized and paralyzed parts
Part ways and seek a higher sky
By our rites through flight
Buy our rights through fight
Our children need to know their identities without bias
And our grandparents without regret
Expect this one fact:

Blood will be shed
Led by the unknown, whose names were renamed
By those whose names are now numbers
By those numbers that are erased from history
We will reclaim them
Unchain them
Untame them
And move forward
So that all people living the "American Dream"
May wake up and see the recurring nightmare of the banished
Brutalized people, uncover your bruises
Victimized people, reveal your wounds
And we will begin to heal
We will be strengthened
Sentence the real criminals to death,
Strap them in an electric chair and deep fry 'til
There's hardly any life left,
Then allow them to choose: Rope or Whip
Though one will be slow and one will be quick,
Both will ensure poetic justice

Oh yes, blood will be shed
And those who fled to Cuba, need flee no more
Panthers will return and hunt down these wolves
We will hold the weapons,
Once owned by Mother Moses and Father Turner
No longer seeking to infiltrate to rebuild
We will set it all ablaze
Burn your white houses and ivory towers
And show this nation's true colors

Show how green earth can be invaded by white faces;
Claimed in the name of red blood, spilled by the indigenous
Brought in brown bodies,
Only to be separated by dark, light, and almost white
Cotton industries constructed to convert green land into green money
It is with this very jade that exalted the red, white and blue
Leaking into salty waters
That we now force them to drink
For too long, they have dined on the taste of their own lies
For too long, they have sipped from the sea of superiority
The rise of the subservient ones will do it
The barrels tap-dancing with racist brain matter will do it
The chopping down of Washington's stone gods will do it
The sounding of the trumpets will do it
Listen for those trumpets
Because once they have sounded,

Blood will be shed

Booking Information

For additional booking information, reading/ speaking appearances, or updates on future events, publications, and workshops...

Email: TheWritePoetry@gmail.com

Facebook: WriteHandedPoet

Twitter: WriteHandedPoet

Instagram: WriteHandedPoet

www.ingramcontent.com/pod-product-compliance
Lightning Source LLC
LaVergne TN
LVHW091308080426
835510LV00007B/414